DANELAW

*A disturbing Story of
British Neo-Nazis ...*

by

PETER HAMILTON

THE CLOISTER HOUSE PRESS

Copyright © 2019 Peter Hamilton

All rights reserved. No part of this publication may be reproduced or transmitted in any form or by any means, electronic or mechanical including photocopying, recording or any information storage or retrieval system, without prior permission in writing from the publishers.

The right of Peter Hamilton to be identified as the author of this work has been asserted by him in accordance with the Copyright, Designs and Patents Act 1988

First published in the United Kingdom in 2019 by

The Cloister House Press

ISBN 978-1-909465-90-9

Foreword

DANELAW is based upon articles in the anti-Fascist magazine SEARCHLIGHT in the early 1990's, which reported an attempt by the neo-Nazi group COMBAT 18 to establish a white-supremacist homeland in East Anglia, with Chelmsford as the capital. COMBAT 18 was then under the leadership of 'Charlie' Sergeant. However, the attempt failed when the party's accountant tried to abscond with party funds and was caught and stabbed to death by Sergeant in a caravan park in Harlow. At the same time as these articles there also appeared in the magazine reports of so-called 'honey-trap' operations by the Secret Service whereby advertisements for new far-right parties were placed in various neo-Nazi magazines and then anyone who applied was placed on record. I combined these two reports into a plot in which the Secret Service decide to set up DANELAW, a whites-only homeland based on the ancient Viking Danelaw of the 9th and 10th centuries, train any applicants into a private army with the apparent intention of attacking mosques, and then at the last minute swoop and arrest them all.

Characters

CLIFF

WARBOYS

GRAHAM

JASON

PAUL

RUTGER

KLAUS

GABRIEL

TARA

ROWENA

ODBURGA

ACT ONE

Scene One

Morning. A prison cell. CLIFF, a big, powerfully-built man in his forties – a genial psychotic giant – is exercising with kettle bells. PAUL, a rough-looking man in his early thirties, is lying dejectedly face down on his bed.

CLIFF Paul. *(Pause)* Paul! What's the matter with you?

PAUL I don't know. Prison blues, I suppose.

CLIFF You have to rise above it. Exercise!

PAUL Exercise? What do you expect me to do? Go for a jog in the fucking park?

CLIFF Don't get cheeky! Or I'll have to drop this weight on your head. Then where will you be? Eh? What did they say to you in Rehabilitation?

PAUL They wanted me to train as a plumber. Apparently there's a shortage of them now in our society.

CLIFF I'm not surprised. Shovelling shit all your life.

PAUL My Dad was a plumber. And he died of a fucking heart attack when he was forty-seven years old. *(Pause)* I'm cold. Are you cold?

CLIFF No.

PAUL You're lucky. I feel the cold. The doctor says I should stop smoking.

Danelaw

CLIFF That's very good advice.

PAUL No ... fuck 'em. I'm a street person, d'you know what I mean?

CLIFF Oh yes. I know what you mean all right.

PAUL I was very into motor bikes. On the outside. I had a Moto Guzzi. Fucking great. What happened was I'd gone down to Brighton for the day – yeh? – and I stops off at a Happy Eater and this cunt starts goading me. For no reason! Spoiling for it. Saying I was a poofter and all this. And as it happened, I still had the helmet in my hand, so I just hit him with it. Battered the fucker unconscious. And he's laying there, blood pouring from his head and that, and his girlfriend's standing there going 'What about me? What's going to happen to me now?' So I took her into the gorse bushes and shagged her and then we both fucked off to Brighton. And we had a really great day. We hit the nudist beach and went swimming in the sea, naked amongst all the queers. It was an enchanted experience. You have to have a little laugh sometimes, don't you? Mind you, they give me two years for it.

CLIFF You were lucky. White man, was he?

PAUL Yeh.

CLIFF You'd have got more for a black or a Paki. I got five years for kicking a Paki's head in.

PAUL That's not fair, mate!

CLIFF I know, but there you are: the cosmopolitan liberal establishment is coming down very heavy on all that sort of thing now. How old are you?

Act One – Scene One

PAUL I'm thirty two years old. Seven of 'em in prison.

CLIFF *(Pause)* I have a little brother – Jason – twenty years old.

PAUL Jason. That's nice. It's like that film: *Jason And The Juggernauts*.

CLIFF Yeh, right. Y'know, when I get out of here, I'm going to go into property.

PAUL Property? What? Like ... houses and that?

CLIFF That's right. I own some waste-land down by the River Lea. It's just a scrap-yard. But it's getting to be worth a small fortune.

PAUL I can believe it.

CLIFF I'm going to mortgage it and then buy some repossessed properties, do 'em up and sell 'em at handsome profit.

PAUL That's very shrewd. I wish I had that sort of organising brain.

CLIFF You see, Paul, with all this debt everyone's getting into now, a lot of people are going to be losing their homes. And I shall just be there, waiting. You could come and work for me if you like. When you've done your time.

PAUL I'd like that very much.

CLIFF You wouldn't need to be too violent. Just a little bit, occasionally.

PAUL That wouldn't bother me. I can be very insensitive sometimes.

CLIFF Eventually I plan to retire to a farm in Cornwall. Or possibly Wales. With my fiancee. You could be my agricultural manager or something.

PAUL I've been to Wales. When I was a kid. Camden Council sent me. Because of my impoverished background. It was to this sort of Adventure Camp. We had to go kayaking and jump over waterfalls. It was very beautiful.

The cell door opens. ENTER WARBOYS, carrying a yellow dossier.

WARBOYS Thank you, officer. Wait a moment, would you? Good morning!

CLIFF Oh yeh? And who are you then?

WARBOYS You don't know me – obviously – but my name is Warboys.

CLIFF You look like one of them things from the Home Office.

WARBOYS Oh dear. I'm sorry to hear that. I take it that you're Cliff.

CLIFF I might be. Depends who's asking.

WARBOYS In that case, you must be Paul.

PAUL That's right, sir.

WARBOYS Well, Paul, I think they want you in the Rehabilitation Unit.

Act One – Scene One

PAUL But I was there only yesterday.

WARBOYS And they want you there again today. So do cut along, like a good chap.

PAUL Oh. Right. Yes. Of course.

EXIT

WARBOYS Thank you, officer! Close the door, would you?

FADE TO BLACK

Scene Two

The same. A few moments later. CLIFF, WARBOYS.

WARBOYS That's better. Now. *(Offers cigarette case.)* Cigarette?

CLIFF I don't smoke. I give it up. I've used my time in prison to develop my body to a very high standard of physical fitness. My body is a temple.

WARBOYS I envy you. My body feels more like a sort of night-club these days. Well, in that case we'll get straight down to the business in hand.

CLIFF Oh yeh? And what business might that be then?

WARBOYS *(Consulting file)* I've been studying your career with great interest.

CLIFF Have you indeed?

WARBOYS Oh yes. I see that you made football hooliganism a very early speciality.

CLIFF *(Modestly)* I received my first conviction when I was fifteen.

WARBOYS What particularly interested us – that's myself and some chums of mine – was the specifically racist nature of your various ... projects.

CLIFF I see.

Act One – Scene Two

WARBOYS I must say, you have been busy. Several attacks on members of the black and Asian communities, culminating in a final assault last March when you fractured the skull of a Pakistani gentleman at a Millwall game. For which you are now serving four years at Her Majesty's pleasure.

CLIFF That is correct.

WARBOYS Plus an extra year for Contempt of Court.

CLIFF That was the judge. He told me I was a racist thug of the worst possible type. So I said to him: Look, Your Honour or Your Worship or whatever the fuck you are, if I'm a racist thug of the *worst* possible type, could you please explain to me what a racist thug of the *best* possible type is? He couldn't answer. Fucker didn't know. Just give me the extra year. Cunt.

WARBOYS That was reckless. I see you tried to get into the Army at one stage.

CLIFF I failed the medical. And I assaulted an Army psychiatrist. He told me I had a severe personality disorder, so I broke his jaw for him.

WARBOYS And after that it was downhill all the way.

CLIFF I've no regrets.

WARBOYS Your father died when you were quite young.

CLIFF He suffered from schizophrenia. He actually died in a mental hospital in Friern Barnet when I was eleven.

WARBOYS I'm sorry.

CLIFF He was always complaining that there was something wrong with his head. He said it had these faulty gears.

WARBOYS Oh dear.

CLIFF And he also claimed that his spinal column had gaps in it. What does that sound like to you? I mean, is there a name for all that?

WARBOYS I don't think so. Faulty gears in the head. I really wouldn't know.

CLIFF No. It's funny, that. Nobody ever does.

WARBOYS Er ... you also have a brother, I believe.

CLIFF Jason. He's actually my half-brother. But I brought him up. I was mother and father to him.

WARBOYS Does he come to see you?

CLIFF No. He finds prisons depressing. Most people do. I don't. I like it.

WARBOYS Hmmmmn. *(Pause)* Now, Cliff, do you think you could explain to me, in your own words, why you dislike black and Asian people so much?

CLIFF Of course I can! It's because they are ruining our country! Just look at this country today. Gangs of fucking blacks roaming the streets with knives and machine guns, for fuck's sake! Warring over drugs and everything. And then there's the mozzies trying to bomb us all to fuck. They are our sworn enemies. And they are deliberately invading us through immigration! They're quite open about it. They want this land for themselves! With all this Sharia Law in place. And they look like getting it an' all. Because it will be handed to them free, on a plate, by a bunch of Marxist-feminist female fucking social workers, who just want to give everything away so they don't feel guilty about the British Empire no more! What a mess! The police daren't do nothing in case they get done for racial harassment or whatever. And these do-gooding liberals are no fucking use. Try telling them about black-on-black gun crime in Bethnal Green, and Pakis in Tottenham building fucking atom bombs in the kitchen, and all they do is start preaching at you about Mosley and the black-shirts! Yeh – fucking Mosley! It's true: any mention of racial tension or anything like that in the East End and it takes your average smug, self-righteous, sanctimonious Liberal-Leftie cunt about nought point three seconds to reach the nineteen thirties! You can practically time the fuckers! It's like it's a nice cosy little theme park for them where they can go and play at being fearless anti-fascists forever!

WARBOYS You've also been involved with the Far Right: Combat 18, the British National Party. Neo-Nazi groups in Holland and Germany.

CLIFF It was mainly in Holland. I had some very dear comrades in Holland. Especially this woman ... I. *(Pause)* But that's all in the past, that is. These days I concentrate more on a sort of recreational violence.

WARBOYS *(Crosses to cell window)* Not much of a view, I must say.

Danelaw

CLIFF Tell me about it.

WARBOYS Let me tell you something about myself first. My name is Terence Charleston Warboys. Of *WARBOYS HALL*, in Gloucestershire. And I can trace my ancestry back to the year eight hundred and sixty six.

CLIFF That is impressive. I've never met anyone who could do that before.

WARBOYS He was called Olaf Clawhand, that first known ancestor of mine, and he was part of the great Danish army that was then busily ravaging a large part of south-east England.

CLIFF Why was he called Clawhand?

WARBOYS Because his right hand was claw-shaped. It's an inherited condition which occurs in many people of Viking blood.

CLIFF Oh. I didn't know that.

WARBOYS Oh yes. Together with a rather more embarrassing condition, which many Viking men also suffered from, which took the form of a rather unfortunate and somewhat unsightly bend in their erect members.

CLIFF Fucking hell. No wonder they was always going berserk.

WARBOYS I merely mention it in passing.

CLIFF It's very interesting. Because I get that in the hand, sometimes. Well, it sort of comes and goes. *(Pause)* And also, but more recently, the er the other thing as well, in fact. That's sort of just started.

Act One – Scene Two

WARBOYS Well, that's very significant. It means you have Viking ancestry.

CLIFF Does it?

WARBOYS Oh yes. You are undoubtedly a Viking by descent.

CLIFF So that's what I am. A Viking. Well I never knew that. So all those people who kept telling me I was a yob and a piece of common gutter scum and a racist thug and all this, they was wrong. Because all the time I was a Viking.

WARBOYS That is what the English are, Cliff: we are the Vikings. And this is our land and it has been ours for a thousand years. So, you see, you're absolutely right to feel as you do. But silly in what you do about it.

CLIFF It makes me feel good. Stamping on some poor fucker of a Paki's face in a nice pair of Doc Martens. It's very delightful.

WARBOYS I'm sure it is. But where does it get you?

CLIFF In prison usually. *(Clasps his head)* Sorry. It's a strange thing, but I get this feeling sometimes that my head has suddenly become very heavy and cumbersome and is about to roll off onto the floor.

WARBOYS That must be very distressing.

CLIFF It is very distressing indeed when you're trying to grow up and there's something wrong with your central nervous system. This bursting head all the time! *(Gives himself complicated manipulations)* That's better.

WARBOYS Good. Now, what would you say, Cliff, if I told you that I and some friends of mine want to change things? What if I said to you that we can get rid of every single black and Asian person in this country?

CLIFF Well, of course, I'd like it very much.

WARBOYS Because that is what we intend to do. We intend to set up a Whites-only English Homeland, which is going to be called the Danelaw.

CLIFF The Danelaw. I like the sound of that. 'The Danelaw'. Yeh.

WARBOYS We are going to build up and train a secret army. Then we are going to seize a substantial portion of East Anglia and declare it to be a Whites-only state. With Chelmsford as the capital.

CLIFF Chelmsford? I know Chelmsford.

WARBOYS I know you do. Your grandparents lived there.

CLIFF I love Chelmsford.

WARBOYS I'm very fond of it myself, of course. *(Pause)* The point is that, in time, we are going to need someone like you.

CLIFF Really? Well, I don't know. The thing is: I do have plans of my own. I was going to start again. With a clean slate.

WARBOYS This would be a clean slate.

CLIFF Anyway I'm going to be locked up in here for the next three years.

Act One – Scene Two

WARBOYS I have some very influential friends and a lot of doors are open to me. *(Nods towards cell door)* Including this one.

CLIFF Well, I don't know. So what would I be then? Supposing I do come.

WARBOYS You'd be a sort of War Leader, initially.

CLIFF A War Leader? Like Churchill. Or King Arthur! I think I'd like that.

WARBOYS I know you would. You're an idealist. You want to serve. That's why you tried to join the Army: you wanted to protect your own people.

CLIFF You're right. I do want to help my own kind.

WARBOYS Now you can. You can give England back to her true people.

CLIFF *(Pause)* All right. Yes. Yes, I would like to be part of all this.

WARBOYS Good man.

CLIFF So what's the next step?

WARBOYS There's still a lot of the logistics to be done. But we shall soon have you out of here. Now, I understand that you own your own business.

CLIFF That's right. It's a scrap metal yard. My fiancee manages it.

WARBOYS This would be Rowena. Does she visit you?

CLIFF Not very often. She's disillusioned with relationships.

WARBOYS Women can be like that. My own first wife ran off with a civil airline pilot over something quite trivial: a perfectly innocent mountaineering expedition with some young Bavarian friends. I'd like to make contact with Rowena. And your brother – Jason – if you think he might be interested. And your cellmate, Paul. Perhaps you could draw me up a list of any of your former comrades who might like to join us.

CLIFF *(A little wary)* Yeh. I can make you a list.

WARBOYS No hurry. All in your own time. Well – goodbye, Cliff.

CLIFF Goodbye.

EXIT WARBOYS

FADE TO BLACK

Scene Three

A sunny morning. A cemetery in the East End. TARA, a girl of seventeen, listening to headphones, sitting on a bench, half in a sleeping bag and drinking SPECIAL BREW and vodka. ENTER JASON, a man of twenty, carrying a bunch of flowers.

JASON Hi.

TARA *(Takes a swig from her can of lager)* Hello there, little soldier.

JASON My name is Jason.

TARA Congratulations.

JASON These are for you.

TARA Thanks a bunch.

JASON *(Puts the flowers on bench)* I shall place them here for you, if I may.

TARA Please yourself. It's a free country.

JASON *(Sits)* I've seen you here a lot.

TARA I've been here a lot.

JASON Your name is Helen.

TARA No it isn't. It's Tara. My name is Tara.

JASON Oh. I thought it was Helen. I must have got you mixed up with someone else.

TARA I think you must.

JASON I used to live on the same estate. I used to see you with your friends.

TARA I haven't got any friends. I'm a loner.

JASON I used to see your Dad about a lot as well.

TARA That's not my Dad. I haven't got a Dad.

JASON Oh. I feel a bit non-plussed by all this.

TARA He's not even my step-Dad. He's not married to my Mum. And he reckons he's my legal guardian! I hate him. He's a bastard!

JASON He is a bit of a drinker, I know.

TARA He's an alcoholic!

JASON Yeh, yeh, I know. An alcoholic.

TARA And he's very handy with his fists. That's why I've started sleeping in a cemetery. He hits my Mum. And me. *(Pause)* And my little brother!

JASON I didn't even know you had a little brother.

TARA He's ten years old. That's why I failed my A Levels – looking after him.

JASON What's he called?

TARA What?

JASON What's he called, your brother?

TARA Erm. I don't know ... offhand.

JASON Oh come along! You must know what your own little brother's called.

Act One – Scene Three

TARA Sammy. He's called Sammy. He still wears short trousers. I love him to bits. *(Pause)* You're the one with the brother in prison, aren't you?

JASON That's my half-brother Clifford. We have the same mother but different fathers. My father is a chartered accountant, I believe.

TARA Oh. Anyway he's some sort of psychopathic racist or something?

JASON No, he's not racist. Although it's true he is a little bit psychopathic. Only quite recently in fact, he kicked in the head of a very unfortunate Asian gentleman at a football match. But it wasn't really racism; it was more like impulsive random violence.

TARA Oh yeh. Of course. *(Drinks)*

JASON He's all right, is Cliff. He's always taken care of me.

TARA That's nice.

JASON Although he did make me accompany him on some of these ... sort of ... football hooligan expeditions he used to organise.

TARA That must have been exciting.

JASON It was, to be honest. All charging along in a big wild gang. I understood it. But I also understood how the Asian fans felt about being attacked. I understand how everybody feels. That's what's so strange. *(Pause)* But what dismayed me was the deliberate attacking of police horses. They threw steel ball bearings to try and make them throw their riders. I hated that. Because I love horses. Especially police horses. I love it when a police-horse van passes and you see those big wise patient heads just looking out.

TARA I like horses.

JASON Would you be terribly shocked if I told you that I am actually quite relieved that Cliff is in prison for a few years?

TARA Nothing ever shocks me. I just like to sort of register it.

JASON That's like me! I like to stand back and observe. Whereas Cliff leans more towards a kind of active participation. It's not true that he's not racist. He does have some racist attitudes. Like he hates all blacks and Asians.

TARA So do a lot of white people. It's not difficult to understand.

JASON I understand it all right! I'm like you. But I don't share his feelings on this issue. I work with them, you see, and it influences you.

TARA *(Suddenly more interested)* Oh? Where do you work?

JASON I work at the B&Q out at Limehouse. I'm in the garden sheds and timber section. And half the chaps on my team are from the Middle East or Africa or the Indian subcontinent. The Team Leader comes from Saudi Arabia. His name is Hafiz. He's very keen on sport and weight training and all that kind of thing. Then there's Mr. Ahmet, the Line Manager. He's my favourite. He wears his spectacles on a leather cord thing. I always

Act One – Scene Three

think he looks like a consultant gynaecologist. Or a barrister perhaps. Or even an Egyptian Professor of Archaeology! I mean, I know nobody welcomes 'em all coming over here but I find that if you're working with people and you get to be on first name terms with them, it's different. I think that if everybody was just all mixed up with each other, and got to know each other personally on these first name terms, everything would come all right. It's just what people are like: they get used to the way things are. *(Pause)* And people find it very satisfying, doing up their houses. The French are getting very keen on it now. I could end up as a manager, living in France. My dream is to buy an old water mill in the Dordogne and completely restore it.

TARA I did French at school for a year. 'J'aime les fleurs! Merci, monsieur.'

JASON I've started to drink red wine. I find I favour the dark wines of Cahors.

TARA I like Special Brew. With vodka chasers.

JASON You could come with me, if you like.

TARA Come with you? Why?

JASON I love you. I want to marry you. I've been thinking about it.

TARA I don't want to get married. This is a bit weird.

JASON I think you're beautiful. I've always thought you was beautiful, Helen.

TARA You hardly know me.

JASON That's not so. I've been watching you for a long time.

TARA I don't want to marry anybody. You must be mad.

JASON No. I just plan things very carefully. Please consider my suggestion. You're wasting your precious young life. With all this drinking.

TARA I'm going through an experimental phase. That's what Life's all about.

JASON What complete and utter nonsense, my dear!

TARA You should try it. Go on – have a slug of vodka, kiddo.

JASON I don't like spirits.

TARA Give it a try.

JASON Very well. *(He drinks some vodka)* You're right. It is extremely nice.

TARA Have some more.

JASON No thank you. I have to be going. I have duties to Society to perform. I hope you consider my proposal, Helen. Tara. I realise it must be a bit of a shock.

TARA It is a bit.

JASON There you are, you see. I knew it was. It's because I understand people. I'm very interested in how they think and feel. It's interesting. I shall return later in the week and find out even more about you. Goodbye, darling.

TARA Yeh, goodbye.

EXIT JASON

FADE TO BLACK

Scene Four

A scrap-metal yard with two caravans and an old Transit van. A double swing seat, large table with pot plants, chairs, junk etc. ROWENA, a rather rough-looking blonde in her early thirties, is peeling potatoes in front of one the caravans. Her dogs – three German Shepherds – suddenly start barking off-stage.

ROWENA Stop that noise! What's the matter with you?

ENTER WARBOYS

WARBOYS Good evening to you.

ROWENA Yeh. Good evening to you an' all.

WARBOYS Sorry about the dogs. I must have startled them.

ROWENA That's all right. They don't like strangers. Quiet!

WARBOYS Lovely dogs, I must say, German Shepherds.

ROWENA Thank you. Do you like dogs?

WARBOYS Oh yes. I'm devoted to animals.

ROWENA That's nice. A lot of people don't like dogs these days.

WARBOYS I know. It's disgraceful.

ROWENA I prefer them to people. That's Stick. Roundabout. And Bufferzone.

Act One – Scene Four

WARBOYS Bufferzone! What a delightful name!

ROWENA That's what he is to me: a buffer zone. So what can I do for you?

WARBOYS Ah, yes. Er ... you must be Rowena, I take it.

ROWENA That's right. How did you know my name?

WARBOYS I know lots of things.

ROWENA I can believe it, an' all. You look intelligent. *(Pause)* Are you wanting to do some business then?

WARBOYS I suppose you could put it like that.

ROWENA Right. I charge thirty quid for a hand-job. You know: masturbation. Fifty quid for straight sex. Seventy quid to suck you off. And a hundred and twenty pounds to take it up the arse. I don't much like that, to be honest. It's fucking painful and it's fucking dangerous these days an' all. But what can you do? It's market forces, innit?

WARBOYS *(Staring at her aghast)* I er ... I think we might be talking at cross-purposes. I was under the impression that you dealt in scrap metal.

ROWENA We used to break up cars. But Brussels ruined all that with these new laws. So we had to diversify. It was an executive decision.

WARBOYS The thing is I'm here more as an emissary.

ROWENA That's all right. So is a lot of my clients. I always wear rubber gloves.

WARBOYS No, no, I mean I have a message from Clifford. Cliff. Your common-law husband. I've been to see him several times in prison.

ROWENA Oh, have you now? Cliff is a good bloke. We go back a long way. So how is he then?

WARBOYS He's very well. The fact is he could well be out of prison soon.

ROWENA What about his five year sentence?

WARBOYS There are ways round that.

ROWENA I'm sorry, but I don't agree with that sort of thing. Justice needs to be done. All these Pakis he's been attacking and committing racism. It's not on. So, are you connected with the Prison Service?

WARBOYS Well, sort of, yes. I suppose you could put it like that.

ROWENA Sort of yes and you suppose I could put it like that. I see. *(Pause)* When will he be joining us then?

WARBOYS A matter of weeks rather than months I should say.

ROWENA I shall look forward to it.

WARBOYS *(Pause)* I've always liked these bleak, marshy, isolated sort of places. I have very fond memories of the Humber Estuary, you know: a sailing holiday with some young Swedish friends. *(Pause)* The River Lea. If memory serves correctly this was the border of the original Danelaw. That could be very. *(Pause)* Well, thank you, Rowena. I must let you get on with your evening.

Act One – Scene Four

ROWENA You're sure you wouldn't like a quick fuck on the house?

WARBOYS It's an intriguing offer but, alas, I must decline on this occasion.

ROWENA A cup of tea, mayhap?

WARBOYS No, thank you. I mustn't detain you. Good night to you. *EXIT*

ROWENA Yeh. And Good-night to you. Officer. I know a copper when I see one.

FADE TO BLACK

Scene Five

A week later. The prison cell. PAUL seated. Enter CLIFF, carrying a sheathed sword.

PAUL What you got there?

CLIFF (*Pause*) This ... (*Unsheathing sword*) ... is a sword. (*He places the blade on PAUL'S neck*) A very sharp sword.

PAUL I can tell that.

CLIFF This is the ancient sword of the Barnstokk. A warrior's sword. It is the sacred weapon of the Nordic peoples.

PAUL That's very interesting.

CLIFF *(Pause)* I hear you've had a little chat with my Mr. Warboys.

PAUL That's right. He summoned me to an interview with him. He was very courteous. He called me Paul.

CLIFF What do you expect him to call you?

PAUL I don't know. Not Paul anyway. It was very nice of him.

CLIFF Well, you're finally moving in more genteel circles, mate. I understand he explained to you about our plans for this country.

PAUL About a Whites-only state? Yeh, he said.

Act One – Scene Five

CLIFF And what do you think to that?

PAUL Sounds like a very good idea to me. What with all these Asians and Arabs and asylum seekers and Romanians pouring in. Fucking asylum seekers! And they're poaching swans now! They're for the Queen, they are.

CLIFF *(Carefully sheathes sword)* You're all right, Paul.

PAUL I know. I'm very loyal and focussed.

CLIFF I'm glad to hear it. And you're quite sure you want to join us?

PAUL Oh yeh! Absolutely. I want to join up all right. Mind you, I was a bit sorry about Wales. But it was only a little twinge of regret.

CLIFF Good. That's all right then . You're in. And from now on I would like you to call me Leader.

PAUL Of course, of course. Leader. *(Pause)* Will I get a uniform, Leader?

CLIFF You will have a uniform and you will be armed.

PAUL Oh yes!

CLIFF In fact, I'm thinking of placing you in charge of national security.

PAUL National security? You mean I'll have my own ministry with a special Interrogation Centre, for interviewing enemies of the state?

CLIFF Yeh. Why not?

PAUL So I can arrest attractive young women on trumped-up charges and take 'em back there, lay them out on special marble slabs, all tied down with leather straps and that, and fuck 'em completely senseless? Whuoooo!

Cell door opens. ENTER GRAHAM, a bewildered, shifty man of about thirty.

GRAHAM *(Very apprehensively)* Hello.

CLIFF *(Pause)* What?

GRAHAM I said ... hello.

CLIFF Did this cunt just say hello to me?

PAUL Yes, Leader.

CLIFF Fucking impertinent cunt!

PAUL Shall I break his arms, Leader?

CLIFF Not just yet. Let's ask him a few questions first. Who are you then?

PAUL Yeh – who are you?

CLIFF Shut up, Paul. Come on – speak up. There's nothing to be afraid of.

GRAHAM Graham. Graham Ellis-Potts. My name is Graham Ellis-Potts.

CLIFF And what are you doing here in my cell, Graham Ellis-Potts?

Act One – Scene Five

GRAHAM I don't know. Governor's orders, I suppose. I'm sorry about it.

CLIFF *(Pause)* I see. *(He looks at PAUL.)* What I meant was: Why the fuck are you privileged to be a guest of Her Majesty? *(PAUL laughs)*

GRAHAM I'm a common thief and fraudster. A betrayer of the public trust. And a person of weak moral character. That's what the judge said anyway.

CLIFF Judges! What do they know ?

GRAHAM This one seemed to know quite a lot. She was a woman as well.

CLIFF I know. They let them do that now. Salt in the wound, mate.

GRAHAM No, she was very accurate. I've made a bit of a mess of things really.

PAUL Join the club. This is a common predicament in here.

GRAHAM *(Tearfully)* I was a Civil Servant. I was with the DSS in Dalston. Arcola Street. I was born and brought up in Hackney and Stoke Newington. I used to work Flexitime. It was very convenient for my part-time Accountancy Course. I've broken Mum's heart!

PAUL Come on, mate. Don't cry. It's unmanly. Think of England.

CLIFF What did you do?

GRAHAM I defrauded the Department by creating false claims. I had the giros sent to my home address.

CLIFF It sounds very ingenious.

GRAHAM I needed the money! I had my Accountancy studies, my writing, I had Mum to look after ... She's in a wheelchair, you see, and I had to do everything for her: dress her, wash her, take her to the toilet.

CLIFF You took your own mother to the toilet?

PAUL You're a hero, mate.

CLIFF I could never do that.

GRAHAM There was nobody else. And now she's disowned me!

CLIFF That's mothers for you. Complete slags. Always dropping fag ash into your Irish stew. *(Pause)* How much longer have you got to go?

GRAHAM A few weeks. When I get out I'd like to concentrate on my poetry. *(Pause)* I write poetry. In my heart of hearts that's what I really am deep down. I like to think of myself as a lower-middle-class poet.

CLIFF Why not working class?

GRAHAM I don't like the working class. I used to! When I was a Socialist I used to hero-worship them. But now I like the lower middle class.

CLIFF *(Pause)* I come from the working class. I'm proud of it.

Act One – Scene Five

GRAHAM *(Pause)* Of course when I say I don't like the working class, it's because I was disillusioned. I worked as a refuse-collector once for Hackney Borough Council and I discovered that working men are not the fearless revolutionary heroes they're made out to be. They're sheep! Moronic, ignorant, cowardly, broken-spirited, yobbish, coarse-minded sheep! That was when I abandoned Socialism as a creed.

CLIFF I hate Socialism. *(Pause)* So, you was brought up in Hackney.

GRAHAM That's right. But eventually the council moved us to Stoke Newington.

CLIFF I was born and brought up in Bow. *(Pause)* Sit down, mate.

GRAHAM Thank you. *(Sits)*

CLIFF What sort of poetry do you write?

GRAHAM I write about people living in dreary suburban wastelands who run away to the countryside to live in a tiny cottage, midst ancient wildwood. *(Takes out notebook)* Perhaps I could read you one. I always have them with me.

CLIFF Go on, then.

PAUL Yeh. Go on. You now have Full Security Clearance.

GRAHAM *(Reads) Oft whilst I dwelt in the city pent,*
Hemmed in by the towering, blank-faced office block
And the blank, unfriendly stare of the so-called city gent,
I would find my dreamy thoughts wandering back

Danelaw

To an oft-imagined, half-known and far-off pleasant
    country
Of densely-wooded hills and flowery green fields,
With fresh, cool streams running down the quiet valley,
Past the snuggling farms, whose harvest yields
All the country dwellers' simple wants ... Then, suddenly,
By an impatient tapping on the glass partition,
I would be rudely jerked back into squalid reality,
And hastily have to remember my official position
As a DSS Clerical Officer, and authorise a payment
To some dirty, smelly, down-at-heel Social Security
    claimant.

(Pause) What do you think?

CLIFF It's quite good. Speaking as someone who loves the countryside and has also claimed Social Security, I think it has something.

GRAHAM Thank you. You don't think I should have shown more compassionate understanding for the claimant?

PAUL No, fuck him. Scrounging cunt.

GRAHAM They do explore a theme that is very close to my heart. I yearn for that long-vanished rural England. But it doesn't exist anymore.

PAUL I think I might be starting to like poetry.

CLIFF *(Dismissing this)* There could be an England like that again one day.

Act One – Scene Five

GRAHAM You can't bring back the past. Reality is urban. Council estates full of immigrants: Nigerians...Turks... Bangladeshis.

PAUL That's right. This is how it all is now.

CLIFF Dare to dream, Graham Ellis-Potts! Dare to dream. I like your writing. I think some friends of mine might like it too.

GRAHAM Poetry is the only thing I've ever cared about. Well, after Mum, of course. *(Taking out photo)* I've got a picture of her here in her wheelchair. She's quite old now, of course. This was taken on Hampstead Heath.

CLIFF Was this before or after you'd taken her to the toilet?

GRAHAM Some time after. I tried to avoid that sort of thing in public. I wasn't allowed to accompany her into the Ladies' to use the facilities. Although, once, in an emergency I did persuade a female traffic warden to go in with her.

PAUL She wiped her arse on a parking ticket! *(Laughs hysterically)*

CLIFF Ignore him. He's a cunt. *(Pause)* I'm going to tell these friends of mine about you. I think they will like you. *(He pats him on the leg)* I like you, anyway.

PAUL *(Ruffling GRAHAM's hair)* So do I, mate. Yeh, you're all right.

FADE TO BLACK

Scene Six

Two days later. The cemetery. Sunday morning. TARA and JASON, drinking vodka.

JASON This is excellent! I read in *The Sunday Times* that vodka is a very pure spirit. It's not like drinking at all. It's actually very good for you.

TARA I can believe it. *(Has a swig of vodka)*

JASON *(Pause)* You know, I've been thinking, ours will have to be quite a long engagement. Until I've established myself in my chosen career.

TARA Yeh. Right. *(Has a second swig)*

JASON You could perhaps work at something during that time and contribute to our joint savings account in the Abbey National Building Society.

TARA Yes, of course. What a wonderful idea, darling! *(Has a long swig)*

JASON When we're married I don't expect you'll need to drink so much.

TARA I might want to drink more. To celebrate. Then there'll be all that French wine an' all. It'll be, like … exploring another culture?

JASON Indeed, yes. We are going to be very, very happy.

TARA *(Pause)* I want to be an actor.

Act One – Scene Six

JASON An actor? Well, that makes me feel very proud of my young wife-to-be. It's very important to know who you are and what you want to do.

TARA This is why I have to experience everything. The flowers in Spring. Sword-fighting. Being a refugee. Being a murderer! Sky diving. Helping people die in a Cancer Hospice. Everything. Also Space Travel if possible. Then I want to go to Hull University and do a degree in Theatre Studies.

JASON I think it's splendid that women have access to Higher Education now *(Pause)* I thought you said that you'd failed your A Levels.

TARA I did. But that don't matter. If you fail your A Levels they have to give you a special scholarship. It's your human rights.

JASON I see. I didn't realise that.

TARA I might have to do very passionate love scenes, when my career takes off.

JASON Oh dear! We'd have to have a very serious marital discussion about that.

TARA Of course! We can always talk it through. *(Takes out bottle of vodka)* Let me give you a little tip, my man! Always carry extra supplies.

JASON Thank you. *(Pause)* I have to say that I am rather worried about you. This is no place for an attractive young woman to be sleeping out in all by herself. There are some very strange people around.

TARA I'd noticed that.

ENTER WARBOYS

WARBOYS Good morning.

JASON Good morning.

WARBOYS You must be Jason.

JASON How do you know?

WARBOYS I know lots of things about you.

JASON Oh. Thank you.

WARBOYS My name is Warboys. If you wish you may call me Terence.

JASON Terence. I think that's a really very lovely name.

WARBOYS How kind of you to say so. Have you been drinking?

JASON No. I don't drink. I mean, yes, I have been drinking but normally I don't drink. Not spirits anyway. Only the dark wines of Cahors.

WARBOYS I see. And what have you been drinking?

JASON Vodka. With my fiancee.

TARA What?

JASON This is my fiancee. Tara. We share a sense of the mystery of things.

WARBOYS I have that sense too. A sense of the Infinite at my shoulder.

Act One – Scene Six

JASON This is it.

TARA Yeh. This is it.

WARBOYS *(Pause)* Now, Jason, I have just come from visiting your brother, Cliff.

JASON Clifford? You've been visiting Clifford?

WARBOYS Yes. There is a possibility that he will be coming out of prison quite soon.

JASON When?

WARBOYS Oh, a few weeks probably. I don't know the exact date.

JASON Well, my goodness me, but that's wonderful news.

WARBOYS There's nothing to be afraid of, you know.

JASON I'm not afraid! On the contrary, I'm overjoyed. My goodness me, yes.

WARBOYS He er he may need your help in a new project.

JASON What sort of new project?

WARBOYS Roughly along the same lines as his old ones, but with more ... political vision. He's going to start a race war. He's going to form a small but highly-trained and well-armed secret militia and he's going to start a race war.

JASON Oh dear.

WARBOYS Do you think you might be interested?

JASON I don't know. Well, of course, yes indeed, I'll be interested. If Cliff is going to be ... I can't not ... I mean, I'll be there for him. Obviously. Oh yes.

TARA I think it sounds exciting and dangerous.

WARBOYS Cliff has asked me to pass on the message to you to meet him at the caravan site and scrap-yard on the Lea River. I'm sure you know where he means.

JASON Yes, indeed. Very much so.

WARBOYS There are ways of getting out of this, if it's what you want.

JASON No, that's fine.

WARBOYS Because youth is sacred. you know. When I was your age I'd climbed in the Himalayas, crossed the Empty Quarter on a camel with a young Iraqui friend, and sailed a thirty-foot ketch single-handedly to New Zealand. That's the sort of thing every adventurous young chap should be doing. *(Pause)* Anyway, I just thought I'd say. I'll be on my way then. Goodbye.

JASON Goodbye, sir.

EXIT WARBOYS

TARA *(Pause)* Can I come with you? To this thingy?

JASON Of course you can.

TARA *(Getting things together)* This is an adventure!

FADE TO BLACK

Scene Seven

Scrap metal yard. ROWENA peeling potatoes. The dogs start barking furiously.

ROWENA Oh no! They're off again! Worse than some poor cow's knickers. What's the matter with you? Mummy's making her nice stew for you all and then she'll give you your dinner. Now shut up! Good doggies. Good doggies!

ENTER JASON and TARA

ROWENA Jason! Hello, darling. Shut up now! Friend! Friend!

JASON Hello, Rowena.

ROWENA You haven't been to see me for a long time.

JASON I'm sorry about that. *(Pause)* This is Tara. My fiancee.

ROWENA Your fiancee. I see. And how are you, darling?

TARA I'm all right, thank you.

JASON A man came to see me. About Clifford.

ROWENA He came to see me an' all.

JASON He said Clifford might be coming out of jail and to meet him here.

ROWENA I'll believe it when I see it.

JASON He said he was going to start a race war.

ROWENA He didn't say nothing to me about it. Mind you, it would be about par for the course for Cliff. He's not exactly fucking Gandhi, is he?

JASON No.

ROWENA I wouldn't pay no attention to it. I don't. Just forget about it.

JASON I find that a bit impossible, to be honest with you. Don't misunderstand me, I love my half-brother Cliff, but ... well.

ROWENA I'm not happy about it either, if the truth be known. It suits me: living here, with him inside. It's the first time in my life I've ever been on my own. I have the dogs. It's nice and quiet at night. I like it.

TARA It is nice here.

ROWENA Well, I'm glad you like it, my lovely

TARA I'd like to live here myself.

ROWENA Well, you can do, my love. You'll be very welcome.

JASON Tara has been living rough in a cemetery.

ROWENA In a cemetery? Oh we can't have that! Here, come and sit down, and make yourself comfortable. Jason, why don't you go and make us all a nice cup of tea while we girls get to know each other.

JASON Of course. I like being useful.

EXIT JASON

Act One – Scene Seven

ROWENA *(Smiles)* Now tell me all about yourself, Tara. How old are you?

TARA Seventeen.

ROWENA Seventeen! And how on earth do you come to be living in a cemetery?

TARA I had to run away from home.

ROWENA Why was that, darling?

TARA *(Pause)* My father, he … he was sexually abusing me. Me and my little brother, Tommy. Sorry: Sammy. Me and my little brother Sammy. *(Amidst sobs she reaches for her vodka)*

ROWENA Dearie me! How dreadful. What's that you're drinking?

TARA Vodka. It's the only thing that takes away the pain.

ROWENA This is terrible: you'd better come and stay here with me, darling. Where you'll be safe and nobody will harm you ever again.

TARA I'd like that.

ROWENA I'm sure you will. Seventeen years old! I'm nearly crying myself here.

TARA Yeh.

ROWENA And what do you want to do in life, Tara?

TARA I thought I might like to be something where I'm helping other people.

ROWENA Well, if you want to help people, and that's a wonderful thing in a young person, you could come and work for me. I'm in the service of others.

TARA What, like social services?

ROWENA That's it exactly. It's like a sort of social therapy what I do. I work with all these refugees and asylum seekers and these economic migrants. I help them get settled in.

ENTER JASON with tea tray

ROWENA I'll tell you all about it later, darling.

TARA I'm going to stay with Rowena for a bit, Jason.

JASON Really?

ROWENA She's coming to help out a bit and stop me getting lonely.

TARA I'm going to train as a social worker. *(She laughs)*

ROWENA That's right. She's going to go to night school.

TARA It could be all part of my project about studying Human Nature.

ROWENA It'll certainly be an education, I can promise you that.

TARA I want to experience everything to do with Life.

ROWENA I know that feeling. I had it once when I was a young girl.

FADE TO BLACK

Scene Eight

A few days later. Cell. GRAHAM and PAUL. ENTER CLIFF.

CLIFF Right, everybody ! I am very happy to report that everything is well under way. *(Looks at GRAHAM)* So we don't have much time for this one. Oh and that reminds me: there has been a new directive from headquarters. My name is no longer to be Leader. I am now to be called Olaf.

PAUL Olaf. I like it. It's got schummn!

CLIFF So. Graham. I believe you've now been to see our prison psychiatrist.

GRAHAM Yes, thank you. Olaf.

CLIFF What did she have to say?

GRAHAM She says she wants to prepare me for my re-entry into society.

CLIFF And when does this happy event take place?

GRAHAM It depends how much remission I get. I like prison. It's because I'm a poet: I can withdraw into the timeless realm of the imagination.

CLIFF You're a strange one. Mind you, I like prison. *(Pause)* Let me tell you about myself. I used to belong to a group of football hooligans. We went round attacking innocent people. They're the best sort. Yeh, we spent our Saturdays charging round the Isle of Dogs or Southampton city centre or wherever, wielding bicycle chains, steering-wheel locks and baseball bats and it was fucking great! Police helicopters circling overhead. We called ourselves *The Limehouse Cutters* and we were having the time of our lives, until I ended up in here. For kicking a Paki's head in. And then something very wonderful happened. A man came to see me. A man with very important connections in business and government. And he told me about these plans of his to build a whites-only state. That is to be called the Danelaw.

GRAHAM The Danelaw?

CLIFF That's right. The Danelaw was the name of an ancient kingdom, ruled by the Vikings. And we are going to take it back. Because that is what we are: Vikings. That is our race. And this is our land. And we want it back. Just like it used to be. No blacks or Asians.

PAUL Yeh!

CLIFF How would you like to join us?

GRAHAM I don't know. Isn't it ... sort of ... racist?

CLIFF No. It's pragmatic.

PAUL Yeh, it's pragmatic.

CLIFF Shut up, Paul. *(Pause)* People like their own kind: it's natural. We stick together. Blacks stick together. And Pakis stick together. We don't think we're better than anybody else. We just want a place to call our own. And they can have a place to call their own. But it won't be round here.

PAUL That's right. They can all fuck off.

Act One – Scene Eight

GRAHAM I don't know ... I know nobody actually likes living in modern Britain. But despite everything, I still like to think that we're all brothers and sisters. Can I just read you a poem I wrote on this very subject?

CLIFF By all means. I appreciate your work.

PAUL So do I. I like things to do with Nature.

CLIFF That's right. He does. Sex and violence mainly.

GRAHAM *(He takes out notebook)* I call it *'The World In Common.'*

(Reads)

I dreamt that I went to Heaven
And it was just like Wanstead Flats:
With fields and woods and sleepy ponds
And dancing swarms of gnats.

And all over the open common
Were happy children playing.
Flying kites and sailing boats, as if
The whole world was a-Maying!

And some of them came from Africa
And some from India and Spain.
And some from other far-off lands
Of which I did not know the name.

But all were happy and at play
And getting on well together.
I'd like the whole world to be like that one day
In such never-ending balmy weather!

PAUL That is very beautiful. That's up there with John Lennon's *'IMAGINE'*.

GRAHAM Thank you.

CLIFF I thought it was bullshit. There'll never be a world like that. Because the strong will always attack the weak. So when you get strong you have to stay that way. Or you will go to the wall. And that's the truth.

PAUL He's right, mate.

CLIFF Of course I'm right. *(Pause)* Anyway, think it over. You don't have to commit yourself right this very moment.

GRAHAM Yes, all right. Of course I'll think about it.

CLIFF We are going to make your dream of England come true. We are going to create the Danelaw exactly as it used to be: an English landscape of woods and fields and hedgerows and little thatched cottages and villages. And I am going to make you our official Warrior Bard. Actually, I might ask you to be the Party's accountant as well.

GRAHAM *(Pause)* I did study Accountancy.

CLIFF I know you did. We shall need someone to administer party funds.

GRAHAM *(Pause)* And you're going to restore the countryside to what it was?

CLIFF Absolutely.

GRAHAM *(Pause)* All right then: Yes.

Act One – Scene Eight

PAUL Well done, mate!

CLIFF Yeh, well done. *(Takes out paper)* Now, I've just got to nip over to Holland for a few days to contact some old friends. Meanwhile you should make your way to this address. It's a scrap-yard and a couple of caravans down by the River Lea. I shall meet you there in about a week's time. And then we shall start to turn this land of ours into a racial bloodbath! All right out there! We are ready!

FADE TO BLACK

ACT TWO

Scene One

A week later. The scrap metal yard. JASON, TARA, ROWENA having afternoon tea.

TARA *(Pause)* I love it here.

ROWENA I'm glad you're happy, my love.

TARA I love all the nettles.

ROWENA I like the nettles.

ENTER WARBOYS, with black leather case. The dogs start barking.

WARBOYS Good afternoon.

JASON Terence! How lovely to see you again!

ROWENA Listen to them dogs! They like you.

WARBOYS I like them. *(Pause)* This is a surprise. I didn't expect to see you here.

JASON I brought my fiancee to stay for a while.

WARBOYS Actually I'd arranged to meet Cliff here today.

ROWENA Clifford's coming?

WARBOYS He should have been here by now. He was released some days ago.

Act Two – Scene One

ROWENA Christ!

WARBOYS I shall just have to wait. What's he been up to I wonder?

ROWENA I wouldn't waste your time worrying about it. Cliff's always been a law unto himself. Do help yourself to a fresh cup of Darjeeling!

PAUSE. ENTER GRAHAM.

GRAHAM Sorry. Have I come to the right place? I was supposed to meet someone called Cliff here. *(Notices ROWENA)* He's a ... he's a political colleague.

ROWENA Join the party. We're all waiting for him.

WARBOYS And who are you exactly?

GRAHAM *(Pause. Gazes at ROWENA)* What? Oh! My name is Graham Ellis-Potts. And until very recently I had the pleasure of sharing a prison cell with Cliff. Er ... I am the Warrior Bard and Chief Accountant of the Danelaw Party.

WARBOYS *The Warrior Bard?*

GRAHAM And Chief Accountant. *(Looking round slowly)* This is nice.

ROWENA Thank you.

GRAHAM You must be Rowena. I've heard about you from Cliff. Looking at you ... it's like seeing a goddess. A wild, free goddess.

ROWENA I've never been told that before.

Danelaw

GRAHAM *(Pause)* And that must be the river!

ENTER CLIFF, PAUL, who carries a wrapped-up sword, baseball bat, ODBURGA, RUTGER, and KLAUS, Dutch Fascists carrying large metal cases. The dogs bark.

CLIFF How charming! A little tea party.

JASON Cliff! Oh this is great, man!

CLIFF Hello, Jason. Home-made orange cake. I've missed this.

WARBOYS Good afternoon, Cliff. I was getting worried about you.

CLIFF There was no need, sir. Everything is under control.

WARBOYS I was just wondering, er who are these guys? And you, madam.

ODBURGA Thank you. *(Smiles at her comrades)* I am glad that you notice.

CLIFF I'll explain shortly, sir. I have some private business to attend to first. *(To the Dutch fascists)* Just give me a few moments. A family matter.

ODBURGA Of course. I am a mother myself.

CLIFF Hello, Jason.

JASON Hey, I've really missed you, man.

CLIFF *(Punches him in the stomach)* In that case ... you should have visited me, shouldn't you? *(Punches him again)* Eh? *(Punches him again)*

Act Two – Scene One

JASON I'm sorry. There were difficulties.

CLIFF *(Punching again)* Difficulties? I'll give you some fucking difficulties!

JASON *(Writhing about on the floor in agony)* I'm sorry. I'm sorry.

CLIFF Stop saying you're sorry! You're sorry, I'm sorry. Everybody's sorry. Stand up. *(Punches him)* There! That's it. It's all over and we'll say no more about it. You are my little brother and I love you.

JASON *(Still writhing in agony)* I love you. I love you.

CLIFF *(Pause)* Hello, Honey-pot.

ROWENA Hello, Cliff.

CLIFF First of all, Rowena, I wish to express my sincere appreciation at the excellent way you have care-takered our joint business venture. Not everyone has your way with scrap metal and that is the simple truth.

ROWENA Thank you. *(Pause)* I did miss you.

CLIFF I missed you.

ROWENA I was meaning to visit but everything got on top of me.

CLIFF I have considered your case very carefully, and I have reached the conclusion that you've got to have all your arms and legs broken.

ROWENA Oh no. Please!

CLIFF You've been on the game, haven't you? you slag!

ROWENA I never! I've had a few guests round sometimes, that's all. In my social life.

CLIFF Social life, my arse! Paul! Baseball bat!

ODBURGA Excuse me. You are going to do this now? Break all arms and legs?

CLIFF Oh yes.

ODBURGA Not good idea. We might need to move quickly after attack on mosque.

WARBOYS *(Very alarmed suddenly)* Attacks on a mosque?

ODBURGA It will be no good if we have a badly-injured person.

CLIFF *(Pause)* All right. We'll put that one on the back burner. *(To ROWENA)* Something for you to look forward to. *(Pause)* So, who's this, then?

JASON This is Tara. My fiancee.

CLIFF No wonder you didn't come and see me. What's your name, darling?

TARA Tara.

CLIFF That's a beautiful name. I haven't seen anyone like you for a long time. I've been in a place where there was no beauty.

TARA That must be dreadful.

CLIFF It is. Dreadful. *(Pause)* You have beautiful hair.

TARA Thank you.

Act Two – Scene One

CLIFF Viking hair.

TARA Thank you.

CLIFF And beautiful eyes.

TARA Thank you.

CLIFF *(Pause)* I hear that you've got a job as well.

JASON I do have a job, yes. Working at B&Q.

CLIFF Working with scumbag Arabs, blacks and Pakis.

JASON It's not like that when you get to know them as individuals.

CLIFF So this is what we've come down to – the proud Viking race. Our raiding parties used to sail their longships up this river, and then come storming ashore to do battle. Later they stayed and farmed the land. For a thousand years. Now look at us. *(Pause)* I'm Cliff.

TARA I know.

CLIFF Like the white cliffs of Dover. Perhaps you can throw yourself over me.

TARA You're a bit wild, aren't you?

CLIFF Oh yeh. Very wild.

TARA I'm wild. They can't handle me at school.

CLIFF Perhaps I could have a try. At handling you.

JASON Yes, as I say, Cliff, Tara and I are engaged to be happily married.

Danelaw

CLIFF That's very nice. You know in Viking lands, when a couple got married the chieftain always got to sleep with the bride on her wedding night.

TARA Oh.

PAUL It was her introduction into the wider Viking community. All the noble Viking warriors got to fuck her in due course.

CLIFF Shut up, Paul. He's only joking.

WARBOYS *(Coming forward)* Look, I really must insist: Who are these people?

CLIFF Of course. These are some Dutch friends of mine. Old comrades. I would like to introduce Odburga, Rutger, and Klaus.

WARBOYS Well, you're very welcome, of course.

ODBURGA I am leader of the group. Some people think women cannot be Fascist. But it is not true. If they can be Communist, they can be Fascist. And to be Fascist is better for a woman. Women are close to Nature and it is natural to have strong national feelings. It is like your family. And I love my family. My children are all life to me.

WARBOYS That's perfectly understandable.

ODBURGA I am a very good Fascist. Since my husband died. He killed himself.

WARBOYS I'm sorry.

Act Two – Scene One

ODBURGA I am the best female Fascist in the Netherlands. Of this I am sure. Though there are more now in Germany, Sweden, Denmark. And Bulgaria. *(Pause)* Rutger is Engineer of our group. Technical Officer.

WARBOYS Good.

ODBURGA And this is Klaus. But he is not political. *(Laughs)* Just crazy.

KLAUS This Danishlaw very good idea!

RUTGER Yes. It is good. In Holland we are now thinking it's time to fight back and get rid of these Muslims. We welcomed them into our country, say it's all right here, everybody's easy-going. But then *they* are not so easy-going. They would even like to stop us drinking.

KLAUS We are very glad to come and fight with you. Although I am not interested in this politics. I just like all the fighting and killing.

PAUL You and me both, mate!

KLAUS Good, mate!

ODBURGA In Holland I am head teacher at my village school. I love my village. I was born there. Things have hardly changed in my village for over three hundred years. My father was a farmer. And my husband. I love my school. But now we are at war with Islam. Everyone knows this. Not many like to admit it, but it is true.

CLIFF We all admit it round here.

ODBURGA The only other people who dare say it are the Israelis. I respect that.

CLIFF Yes. It may seem a bit ironic, considering that we are all neo-Nazis, but I must confess to a grudging admiration for the Israeli Army. They don't fuck around. Look at that Rachel Corrie. She goes over there, thinking she can save the world and all that, and they run her over with a fucking bulldozer! Some other cunt an' all. In Rafah. Israeli sniper took him out with a head shot at two hundred yards. Oh yes! We are all Israelis now.

ODBURGA That is the truth. We are all Israelis now.

RUTGER I had a very good job with a big Dutch corporation. I had a nice house. Family. Then I was made redundant. So I started drinking a lot of Scottish whisky. Then my wife ran off with a dentist. Yes, a dentist! And she takes the children with her. But that was O.K! I thought: Good! I am free! I can do something with my life. So I joined the Dutch National Socialist Party. To fight these Muslims. So yes, we are all Israelis now.

TARA I'm hungry for adventure. I want to go to these places you read about. Lebanon ... Haifa. And Petra! And I want to go up the River Nile and see the Pyramids. And Japan and China. And Australia! *(Swigs vodka)* So, yeh, we are all Israelis now! Why not indeed?

CLIFF That is so youthful and lovely. *(Pause)* Right now though, we've got more urgent matters to discuss. Show 'em what's in the cases, lads.

Act Two – Scene One

KLAUS *(While they all open cases)* Ten Heckler Koch submachine guns. The best. All brand new. Each with two thousand rounds of ammunition.

RUTGER Twenty automatic pistols. Each with five hundred rounds of ammunition.

ODBURGA Thirty rocket-propelled grenades with two launchers.

KLAUS One hundred hand-grenade. Very powerful. Make big mess in crowd.

WARBOYS Oh dear.

CLIFF What?

WARBOYS Nothing. I mean, what's it all for?

CLIFF We are going to start a war!

WARBOYS But where did you get these weapons?

RUTGER It's easy to buy weapons in Europe today. After war in Balkans.

WARBOYS *(Sitting down)* Christ!

CLIFF What's the matter?

WARBOYS I'm a little surprised, that's all.

CLIFF I thought you'd be pleased.

WARBOYS Of course I'm pleased.

CLIFF You said something about money at our last meeting.

WARBOYS Yes. And here it is. *(Opens case)* Party funds, as promised. Four hundred thousand pounds.

GRAHAM Four hundred *thousand?*

CLIFF This money will be your responsibility. As Party Accountant.

GRAHAM Of course. I'm not afraid of responsibility. *(He takes the case)*

CLIFF You know why we are here. It's to establish a whites-only homeland in East Anglia. With Chelmsford as the capital. This homeland is to be called the Danelaw. So it's a very historic occasion. *(Pause. Holds head)* And this is Mr. Warboys, whose idea it was, and he is head of a consortium which has got interests and investments in oil and armaments and all like that.

JASON Right. I see. Yes.

CLIFF And over the next few months we are going to train up a secret army. I understand this will take place at a special training camp in Norfolk.

WARBOYS That is correct.

CLIFF That is correct. And when we have been transformed into an elite fighting unit, we are going to seize all the lands along the East Coast up to the Humber and declare it to be the new Danelaw. We are going to light a flickering candle in a darkened England and the flame is going to get stronger and stronger and it will be the undying flame of the Northern Folk! *(He holds his head with both hands and down his back)* Sorry. It's my spinal

Act Two – Scene One

cord: it's being used to transmit radio messages by GCHQ Cheltenham. This is what they can do to you. *(Pause)* Where was I? Oh yes. But first we have to set up our Headquarters, from where we can conduct a recruitment campaign. But before then – and this is the good bit – because it will take some time for Graham, our Party Accountant, to arrange the purchase of a suitable property, what with exchanging contracts and mortgages and all that bureaucratic shit, we are going to start livening things up a bit on our own. We are going to attack a few Paki shops, nightclubs where all the blacks go ... And then a mosque. That will be the main target.

PAUL An excellent idea, Olaf. Keep up morale.

CLIFF Thank you, Paul. So what I want now is for you all to go to Chelmsford together and look for a suitable property to be our Party Headquarters. All except Tara who I need to remain here for er strategic reasons.

GRAHAM And I shall deposit this money safely in the Halifax Building Society.

CLIFF That's a very good idea.

ROWENA Well, I'm going to take the dogs to my Mum's. *(All the dogs start barking)* Yes! You're going to Nanna's for a little holiday, aren't you?

GRAHAM I shall accompany you. If I may.

EXIT ROWENA, GRAHAM

JASON I'm sorry ... but I think that Tara should really come with me.

CLIFF I'm afraid that won't be possible. Because of logistics. Tell him, Paul.

PAUL Yeh, I'm sorry, mate, but that information is classified. For Security reasons. I'll explain all this on the way.

EXIT PAUL, JASON.

WARBOYS Look, I'm afraid that all this is far too premature. We should concentrate on recruitment and training. There's a great deal of planning involved in a venture of this nature.

CLIFF I want to start with a nice big bang.

WARBOYS Right. Yes, I see. Right, okay, yes, that's fine. Look ... I er I really do have to be going. There are people I have to see quite urgently.

CLIFF Of course. No doubt you'll be making contact again soon.

WARBOYS You can count on it.

EXIT

CLIFF And also you three comrades. I'd like you to go and ... erm ... secure the perimeter and that.

ODBURGA Of course. Follow me, guys.

EXIT ODBURGA, RUTGER, KLAUS.

Pause. TARA inspects the weapons. She picks up a grenade.

TARA This is a bit scary.

CLIFF You like it though, don't you?

Act Two – Scene One

TARA I do a bit. It's adventurous.

CLIFF You need never be scared of me.

TARA I know. Anyway I don't mind being racist for a bit. As an actor, I have to know how everyone feels.

CLIFF Of course you do. *(Caresses her)* How would you like to be a queen?

TARA I don't agree with royalty at the moment. I'm a Communist.

CLIFF You can be my Viking queen. The Danelaw is women. Women are a sacred mystery who all live in the centre of the world in a cave in a wood round a big log fire and they stir the pot and sing and dance naked in the firelight.

TARA I think I might like that.

CLIFF We English are losing our culture. Everybody else is allowed their own culture except the English, have you noticed that?

TARA I had, sort of.

CLIFF Well, we want it back!

TARA It sounds exciting.

CLIFF It is exciting. Vikings are never bored. It's a scientific fact.

TARA I want to dance in the firelight at the centre of the world. I want to be naked.

CLIFF You shall be naked. *(He starts to undress her)* Now, as I remove your clothing, I want you to imagine that you are standing under a sacred waterfall. And all around you are the rocks and trees and skies and rivers of our Northern land. It is like the first morning on Earth, and the sun is rising.

TARA Yeh, the sun is rising! And thou must do with me as thou wisheth!

CLIFF I shall enjoy that.

FADE TO BLACK

Scene Two

WARBOYS alone, on mobile.

WARBOYS Weapons! That's what I said. They've got weapons and they're planning to attack a mosque. In a few days! Yes! We have very little time if we want to mount some kind of operation. Two or three days at the most. What? Well they're armed to the bloody teeth. RPG's, sub machine-guns, automatic pistols, hand grenades, the lot. That's right, Dutch Nazis. We did know he had contacts in the past, but he told me he'd finished with it. What? Well, I think we should get our best people out and hit them as soon as possible. We can't risk a mosque being attacked. It doesn't bear thinking about. It's not so bad, Sherwood. This will just be a much quicker result, that's all. Look on the bright side: we can blame the whole thing on the bloody Dutch. Anyway I'd better get back there and keep an eye on the situation and you can start the ball rolling at your end. Out.

FADE TO BLACK

Scene Three

Afternoon. A day or so later. Caravan site. TARA seated, drinking whisky. There is a Nazi-style banner, with the double lightning flash of the Sowela rune. ENTER JASON

JASON *(Pause)* Hi.

TARA Hello there, tosh!

JASON *(Pause)* Where's Cliff?

TARA I don't know. Never ask a Viking where he's been or where he's going or what time he's coming back. It drives 'em fucking crazy. *(Pause)* My name is Inglis now. That's a Norse goddess. Inglis.

JASON *(Shakes his head)* A Norse goddess. What about your career?

TARA That's all in hand.

JASON I thought we were engaged.

TARA We are engaged.

JASON So what about France then?

TARA France is great. I love France. J'aime La France!

JASON Have you been unfaithful with him?

TARA Of course I haven't! He wants to wait till I've done my A Levels. It's a Viking law. I'm Queen of the Danelaw now. I am going to sit on a great wooden throne carved from a single old giant oak tree, and all the fearless

Act Two – Scene Three

warriors of the Northern Folk are going to lay their golden spears at my feet in homage.

JASON Look at all this. This is going back to Hitler.

TARA No, it isn't. You're just showing your ignorance. That's the Sowela rune, that is: the Nordic rune for the sun. It gives us a sacred power.

JASON I feel cold. I can't understand it. It's a sunny day. *(He curls up on the floor)*

TARA Jason! You can't go to sleep here!

JASON I feel cold. I'm tired.

TARA I shall make you feel better. *(Takes out sword)* I can heal you. I've been given healing powers by the Spirits of the North. They were given to me in a special ceremony by Olaf. With this sword. The ancient sword of the Barnstokk! *(Pause)* I heal thee. I heal thee in the name of the North Wind. I heal thee in the name of the sacred trees of the Northern Land. I heal thee in the name of the sacred Northern river. And I heal thee in the name of the wolf, I heal thee in the name of the great wild boar and I heal thee in the name of ... *(Pause)* ... Oh dear! I've forgotten what the other one was now. Fuck! It was either the eagle or the salmon, I know that. I heal thee in the name of the eagle. And the salmon. *(Pause)* It's going to be so beautiful, Jason, where we're going. The rocks and the pine trees and the wolves and the eagles and the blue sky and the roar of the waterfalls and rivers. And the sea. *(Pause)* It'll start to work soon. You will feel the sacred sun energy, like a great golden fire, going all up your spine. And you will feel the sacred power of the drawn sword of the Barnstokk in your hand. And then you will go out into the world and make everything just how you want it.

JASON No. You don't understand.

TARA Jason! Look, I've got to go soon. I'm going to a picnic!

FADE TO BLACK

Scene Four

Later. The same. ROWENA peeling potatoes and crying. ENTER GRAHAM.

GRAHAM *(Pause)* What's the matter?

ROWENA He's going to do for me this time. You have no idea what he's capable of.

GRAHAM *(Pause)* You're peeling potatoes.

ROWENA I had to do something to take my mind off it all.

GRAHAM You look like a Gypsy.

ROWENA I wish I was a fucking Gypsy. I'd be out of here like a shot.

GRAHAM I love Gypsies. The true Romanies. *(Pause)* Where is everybody?

ROWENA I don't know. There's nobody here. He's gone off with that Tara.

GRAHAM *(Pause)* What do you think of this Danelaw thing?

ROWENA *(Wary)* Well, I think it's very interesting.

GRAHAM Really?

ROWENA Yes. I mean, I don't know. What do you think?

GRAHAM I utterly condemn it. As a humanist poet, I believe in the Brotherhood of Man. There's nothing I can do about it though. We poets can only gaze upon the follies of mankind and weep.

ROWENA I'm more worried about what he's going to do to me. He's going to break all my arms and legs.

GRAHAM *(Pause)* Look, if you want, you can come away with me.

ROWENA What?

GRAHAM If you like, you can come away with me. That's why I came back.

ROWENA For me?

GRAHAM Yes.

ROWENA You came back to rescue me?

GRAHAM Yes.

ROWENA *(Pause)* Where are you going?

GRAHAM Croatia.

ROWENA Croatia! How the fuck are you going to get to Croatia?

GRAHAM *(Pause)* You know the four hundred thousand pounds he gave me? I've still got it. And I'm going to keep it.

ROWENA You must be insane. He'll cut you into little pieces when he finds out.

GRAHAM It was clearly my moral duty to liberate this money from the grip of International Fascism and place it in the service of Humanity. *(Pause)* So, instead of going to the bank, I bought a Volkswagen camper van.

Act Two – Scene Four

ROWENA And you're going to go to Croatia in it?

GRAHAM Yes. It's a beautiful, unspoilt country: thousands of square miles of forest and mountains and lakes where you can buy farms really cheap. I intend to rear chickens and grow organic vegetables, while I write my poetry warning everybody about climate change and racism.

ROWENA You're as mad as everybody else round here.

GRAHAM Like all poets I practise an enlightened and noble selfishness.

ROWENA Why are you telling me all this?

GRAHAM *(Pause)* I have loved you from the very first moment that I saw you; here, by the river.

ROWENA Oh. I see.

GRAHAM I know it must sound silly.

ROWENA No, not at all.

GRAHAM I was wondering ... what do you feel about Cliff?

ROWENA Fear. *(Pause)* There was a bond between us once. But not now.

GRAHAM Then come with me to Croatia.

ROWENA I couldn't.

GRAHAM It's your only hope. Once this Danelaw thing starts all hell is going to break loose. The police will be all over this place.

ROWENA *(Softly, fearfully)* Oh Christ. I don't want to go to prison.

GRAHAM Of course not. You're a free spirit. *(Pause)* So what do you say?

ROWENA I don't know. I'll have to think about it.

GRAHAM The trouble is there's no time to think.

ROWENA *(Pause)* All right. I'll come.

KLAUS, RUTGER and ODBURGA appear as if from nowhere behind them, armed.

ROWENA It's all over, I know.

ODBURGA Yes. All over. Sit down now, back to back and put your hands on top of head! Or we kill you. Very quiet. No-one will hear shots.

ROWENA Oh Christ! Oh Jesus Christ!

ODBURGA He cannot help you anymore.

ROWENA What have I done?

ODBURGA I think you have killed yourself. Sit. *(They sit)* Rutger.

RUTGER Yes?

ODBURGA You ring Clifford.

RUTGER *(Dials on mobile.)* Hello? Cliff? Yes, Rutger here. I have bad news.

FADE TO BLACK

Scene Five

Epping Forest. Same time that afternoon. CLIFF, TARA having picnic.

CLIFF This is nice.

TARA Yeh. It is.

CLIFF I've always liked trees.

TARA I like trees.

CLIFF I'd like to live in a great big forest one day.

TARA Yeh. So would I.

CLIFF Then you shall.

TARA *(Pause)* Can I say something?

CLIFF You can always say whatever you like to me.

TARA It's just that, although I have enjoyed my time as a fascist and Norse goddess, it's time to move on. I want to go home to Mum and Dad.

CLIFF *(Pause)* I shall drive you there.

TARA *(Pause)* You don't mind?

CLIFF No.

TARA I've been accepted on a Theatre Studies course at Hull University.

CLIFF That's excellent news. Education is the only hope for people like us.

Danelaw

TARA *(Pause)* Are you really going to start a race war?

CLIFF Oh yes.

TARA But, I mean, won't people get killed?

CLIFF That's what happens in a war.

TARA I understand how you feel. I understand how everybody feels. That's what actors have to do. But I think that everybody should just chill out a bit! I mean look at them all in that Gaza and Syria and Afghanistan or wherever, all bombing each other to fuck. What's the matter with 'em? Why can't they just enjoy life and get on with each other?

CLIFF I used to be like you. Oh yes. Off I toddled into the world with a great big smile on my face and sunshine in my heart. In my heart! *(Pause)* There's going to be years of war and killing. I now have a very clear vision of the Danelaw. First we have to burn down all the cities. The cities will be reclaimed by Nature. Then, when the wars are over and we've kicked out all the blacks and Pakis, we shall abolish firearms. The Danelaw is to be a land of fierce warriors who only fight with the great broadsword and the iron-tipped spear and the mighty war-axe. And every man shall have his own land. When he comes home on winter evenings he will see the lights of his homestead in the gathering twilight. And men will ride horses again.

TARA I like horses.

Act Two – Scene Five

CLIFF *(Mobile rings).* Will you excuse me a moment? Hello? Rutger! What can I do for you, mate? Sorry – could you say that again? I see. In that case I shall return immediately. *(Pause)* It's all starting.

FADE TO BLACK

Scene Six

LIGHTS UP on TARA, at Hull University, a year later. In front of a white screen.

TARA I had nothing to do with any of what happened that night. *(Pause)* I was going to telephone the papers. I'd made my mind up. First thing in the morning. I had the coins and everything. I was going to ring the *SUN*. I'd have been a hero. *'Promising Young Actress Prevents Racist Massacre.'* Oh yeh. But we could hear it all going on. With the police helicopter and everything. And next day it was on the television news. *(Pause)* Anyway I was lucky in the end. I got away with it. Because that sort of stuff can stick to you. And you know how officious everybody is now. *(Pause)* I love being at university. We work very hard on the Theatre Studies course, because of all the practical. And Mum and Dad have been up to visit and I showed them round the campus. And round the historic medieval centre of Hull. *(Pause)* They came to see me in our end-of-year production, *MIDSUMMER NIGHT'S DREAM*. I played Helena. Which was good. Because that's like my name. Helen. Everyone said it was a very vibrant production. It was set in a Marks and Spencers. And Theseus was the manager and Helena and Hermione and all them, they were all these asylum seekers. And they all run off to the staff roof garden, where the fairies live, and have sex. It was great! And next year there's a group of us going to get a flat together in Hull. *(On screen a picture of the First Year Theatre Studies Undergraduates, all smiling happily.)*

FADE TO BLACK.

Scene Seven

Later. The cemetery, as in Scene Three. JASON seated. ENTER WARBOYS

WARBOYS There you are, Jason. I've been looking everywhere for you. I suddenly thought: the cemetery. That's where he'd go.

JASON *(Pause)* I've packed my job in.

WARBOYS Oh dear. Why is that?

JASON It wasn't going anywhere. I was kidding myself. There isn't going to be a watermill in Provence. No vineyard. *(Pause)* No marriage. *(Pause)* It's Cliff ... my brother Cliff! ... he's fucked my fiancée!

WARBOYS Oh dear. You poor sweet boy. Look, I know that now you think you'll never get over it, but I promise in time you will.

JASON No, I won't. Never.

WARBOYS Why don't you come down to *WARBOYS HALL* for a few days?

JASON *WARBOYS HALL?*

WARBOYS My estate in Gloucestershire. Do you like horses?

JASON Yes, of course, sir. I love all animals.

WARBOYS We have lots of horses. You can come and ride them.

Danelaw

JASON No. I have to sort things out. I shouldn't have just walked out like that. And this *DANELAW* thing an' all. What's Mr. Ahmet going to say?

WARBOYS I wouldn't worry about *DANELAW*, if I were you. I can assure you, with absolute certainty in fact, that in just a few hours from now it is going to come to a very violent and untimely end.

JASON How do you know?

WARBOYS *(Pause)* I'm not supposed to tell you this. But I work for the Government.

JASON I thought you was a business entrepreneur.

WARBOYS I work for the Secret Service. My Department monitors all the loonies of the Left and Right: Combat 18, the BNP, the Workers Revolutionary Party. We keep an eye on them all.

JASON I see.

WARBOYS We call this a honey-trap operation in the trade: we set up a bogus neo-Nazi Party, advertise for recruits, and see what we catch. We were going to form a small private army, and take them to a camp in Norfolk for combat training. Go through the motions of planning attacks on Muslims. Then at the last moment we swoop, bag the lot and bang them up in Belmarsh for thirty years. It would have been a masterpiece of public relations.

JASON Oh. I must say, it does seem rather unfair to lead people on like that. They might never have done nothing about it otherwise. It's what people are like. They're all over the place.

WARBOYS You're obviously a very sensitive and thoughtful young man.

JASON Thank you, sir.

WARBOYS Anyway, these atrocities they're planning simply aren't going to happen. In fact in only a few hours from now they are going to be visited by some very efficient men indeed and it's all going to get very bloody. I wasn't supposed to tell you this but I did. And so you see, what you have to do is come with me. You are now officially a security risk, I'm afraid.

JASON Of course. I understand.

WARBOYS You don't realise just how wonderful life can be, you know. And I think you deserve a chance to find out.

FADE TO BLACK

Scene Eight

The caravan site. Later that evening. GRAHAM and ROWENA seated, bound, on kitchen chairs. SR CLIFF is sharpening a broadsword. PAUL is standing guard over ROWENA. ODBURGA, KLAUS, RUTGER – all armed.

ROWENA *(Whimpering)* Please, Cliff. I don't want to die.

CLIFF Nobody ever does. I don't understand it. Life is such shit, you'd think they'd be glad to go. But no. And stop all that whining. Shut her up, Paul.

PAUL Shut the fuck up! *(Punches her unconscious)* She's shut up, Olaf.

CLIFF Thank you. This is the ancient sword of the Barnstokk. It is a Viking broadsword. And because it is a warrior's sword, every so often it must taste blood. *(Puts it against Graham's neck)*

GRAHAM It's very sharp.

CLIFF You're a very observant man, Graham. It must be the poet in you. *(Puts sword down and opens briefcase)* You betrayed us. For money.

GRAHAM It was in a weak moment of greed and selfishness. It's what we writers call a fatal character flaw.

CLIFF Really? *(Takes out sheet of paper)* What's this?

GRAHAM It's my latest poem. I call it *'The Gypsy Woman.'* It's the best thing I've ever done actually. It all came out

Act Two – Scene Eight

in a single sustained rush. It's dedicated to Rowena. You can read it if you want.

CLIFF What about you, Paul? Do you want to hear Graham's latest masterpiece?

PAUL Certainly, Olaf. I appreciate his poetry.

CLIFF Here – you read it.

PAUL *(Reads)*

I met a gypsy woman
Living on the wild, wild moor.
She was busily peeling potatoes
By the caravan door.

Her hair was a field of ripening corn
Waving in the summer breeze.
Her eyes were like blue summer skies
Above the deep and sparkling seas.

I said to her:'Gypsy woman,
I must come and live with you.
I must lay my head on your large firm breast
And swear to be always true.'

So she called her horse from the meadow –
It was a big brown mare called Bess –
And we drove off together down the rough moorland road
And I resigned from the DSS.

ODBURGA You know, that is quite good. I would give that high mark in my class.

RUTGER I love all the Arts. I like opera very much. Puccini. *La Boheme*!

CLIFF But Rowena's not a gypsy. She's a slag. Once she was everything to me. *(Takes sword)* I shall open you up with surgical precision, I think. And then, with an almost deliberate clumsiness, I shall slowly hack your heart out.

GRAHAM No, please. *(CLIFF stabs him. Graham dies.)*

ODBURGA Good God! This is butchery! To kill like that. We are not monsters. I thought I knew you.

KLAUS *(Speaking low to RUTGER)* I like this guy. He's like me.

RUTGER I think you are right.

PAUL *(Pause)* He's dead.

CLIFF That's right, Paul. *(He crosses to ROWENA)*

PAUL She's still unconscious.

CLIFF That's good. I don't want her to suffer unduly. I shall go in discreetly under the rib cage and so up into the heart.

ODBURGA But why not just shoot them? It is kinder.

KLAUS It is more fun this way.

CLIFF *(He starts to stab ROWENA slowly. She wakes and starts screaming in agony. She dies. To PAUL)* What's the matter with you?

PAUL I'm not feeling very well.

Act Two – Scene Eight

CLIFF You knew people were going to die.

PAUL Yeh, but not like this. I thought it would be more, like, in noble battle.

CLIFF *(He approaches ODBURGA)* I'm sorry you had to witness such a brutal scene. I've just remembered how sensitive you are.

ODBURGA Thank you.

CLIFF I was genuinely sorry to hear about your husband. I liked him.

ODBURGA He lost his farm. He could not fight anymore.

CLIFF The thing is, now that I'm free, Odburga, and you are, I was thinking that perhaps, you and me, we could get together perhaps.

ODBURGA Oh.

CLIFF None of this is going anywhere, you know. England is finished.

ODBURGA This is what you think?

CLIFF All the nation states are on their way out. This European Union thing's going to be everywhere. It'll be like Communist China.

RUTGER I have thought this too.

CLIFF One big all-powerful state. Everybody controlled. No individuality.

KLAUS If this comes to happen I shall be a bandit in the mountains.

Danelaw

CLIFF I've been thinking – I'd like to get a boat. Out on the ocean, you can still be a free man. Despite all this plastic. I'd very much like you to come with me.

ODBURGA I don't think so. I have my children. They are growing up now.

CLIFF We could sail to the Cape Verde Islands. And the Azores.

ODBURGA I will maybe think about it.

There is a helicopter above and a searchlight. A voice through a loudspeaker.

VOICE Armed police – Put down your weapons! Put down your weapons!

PAUL *(He collapses with chest pains)* This is it for me.

KLAUS We fight now, boys! We fight now to the death! This is greatness!

RUTGER That very bad wife Maartje will read about me perhaps, in the newspapers. Well, I hope she's happy with her very stupid dentist!

ODBURGA My school. It will be short of a teacher soon, I think.

VOICE *(Pause)* I repeat: Armed police – put down your weapons! *(CLIFF does so)* Now put your hands on your head. And stand still!

KLAUS OK! Now! This is greatness! This is greatness!

Act Two – Scene Eight

There are prolonged bursts of gunfire. The three Dutch fascists are killed one by one.

CLIFF *(Pause)* Paul? *(Pause)* Paul! Odburga!

ENTER WARBOYS.

WARBOYS They're all dead. And this is ours, I believe. *(Takes briefcase)*

FADE TO BLACK

Scene Nine

Drawing Room at WARBOYS HALL. WARBOYS listening to Elgar. ENTER JASON with jug of champagne cocktails and glasses.

JASON Here we are, sir! I've prepared some delicious French Seventy-fives.

WARBOYS Jolly good!

JASON Who would have thought of mixing gin and champagne? It's genius.

WARBOYS It is. What a truly great man he must have been! And only a man could think of it, you know. Women don't have that daring creative spark.

JASON I must say I do find a bottle of excellent champagne most refreshing.

WARBOYS *(Pause)* You like it here, don't you?

JASON I do, sir. *(Pause)* I was just wondering though about Cliff. Is he dead?

WARBOYS No. He's not dead. But he has been detained in a special facility we have on the South Down; where he's being treated with a carefully-balanced mixture of drugs, hypnosis, and electric shocks. Although, to be absolutely honest, I think the electric shocks are a minor self-indulgence on the part of his medical team. Yes, I'm afraid it has to be admitted that, seventy years ago, some

Act Two – Scene Nine

of the people we employ there would have been probably been put on trial at Nuremberg. *(Pause)* His mind has completely gone, you know. But he'll be kept there and cared for quite humanely for the rest of his life.

JASON That's good. I mean, it's not that I don't ... it's just that ... *(Stops)*

WARBOYS You can stay here as long as you like, you know.

JASON Thank you.

WARBOYS I must say you do ride very well.

JASON I love horses.

WARBOYS Most people do, in their heart of hearts. *(Pause)* I think I'd like to show you India. We can start off in Rajasthan. Then cross into the Pradesh to Agra. See the Taj Mahal. And then up into the foothills of the Himalayas to visit the old British hill stations, and finally on into Nepal, where I can introduce you to some of my old Gurkha chums. Best soldiers in the world. I served in the Seventh Battalion, the Gurkha Regiment as a young man, you know.

JASON It sounds magic.

WARBOYS Then we could go sailing in the Southern Ocean.

JASON Yes, sir. *(Pause)* The thing is though ... I think I really ought to be getting back to the B & Q out at Limehouse.

WARBOYS I thought you'd 'given in your notice' or whatever it's called.

JASON No. I just disappeared. Without saying nothing. I could go back. I'm sure Mr. Ahmet would understand. It's difficult to explain ... but I fitted in. It's where I belong. I keep thinking about everybody.

WARBOYS We all have to burn our bridges sometimes.

JASON Mr. Ahmet will be taking delivery soon of the new Swiss-Chalet-style range of garden sheds. They all have little verandas and steep cottage rooves and everything. They're brilliant. And you have a choice of four colours: Apple Red, Mustard Yellow, Summer Sky Blue and Nettle Green.

WARBOYS Perhaps we could order some for *WARBOYS HALL*.

JASON I don't think so.

WARBOYS No, neither do I. Elspeth would have a fit.

JASON I think it's the way forward. Everybody all mixed up together and living on nice orderly estates. All doing their homes up and everything. Everybody all friendly and being nice to everybody else! Cheerfully greeting each other by their first names across the garden fences. Hello, Azi! Or Zihni or whatever. Or Dave! A lot of black guys are called Dave now, have you noticed that?

WARBOYS I must confess that it hadn't leaped out at me.

JASON Just in my last week we had a new guy started in

Act Two – Scene Nine

the Household Paint Section called Dave. He was a black guy. His family come from the West Indies. He was in charge of the paint mixer. Because you can choose your own colour and they mix it up for you. To make it unique. That's what people like. And then, almost the next day it was, we had a new postman making the morning delivery and he was another black guy and when I asked him his name it turned out he was called Dave an' all. That's how things are.

WARBOYS I must say, you're a most refreshingly strange young man.

JASON Thank you. I like to think about things in my own way, that's all. I think maybe I should go back. It's where I belong.

WARBOYS No more horses? No sailing across the Southern Ocean? No camping out in the deserts? No French Seventy-fives?

JASON Perhaps you're right. *(Gazing out of window)* It wouldn't be as nice as here. This is beautiful. I love anything to do with animals and Nature.

WARBOYS What healthy young man doesn't?

JASON *(Regretfully)* You're right. You're right. There's no going back.

FADE TO BLACK

Scene Ten

The gardens of a top-secret mental institution. ENTER CLIFF, clutching a toy dog, with GABRIEL, a black PSYCHIATRIC NURSE who is carrying a Law book.

GABRIEL *(Guiding CLIFF)* All right, mate?

CLIFF Yes. I'm all right. I'm all right. I'm very happy, actually.

GABRIEL *(Sits, opens book.)* Good.

CLIFF This is a very beautiful place.

GABRIEL It is, isn't it? We're very lucky.

CLIFF I feel I could spend the rest of my life here.

GABRIEL I think that may be just as well, mate.

CLIFF *(Pause)* You're reading a book!

GABRIEL Yeh.

CLIFF I love books! I've never read one as big as that, though!

GABRIEL This is a Law book. I'm studying the Law. Part-time.

CLIFF That's excellent. Education is the key to everything.

GABRIEL I think so.

Act Two – Scene Ten

CLIFF I once had a young female friend who I encouraged to go to University. After I'd fucked her a few times.

GABRIEL Right. What was she studying?

CLIFF I can't remember. Architecture, perhaps. Or Biology. Or ... maybe Archeology. Maths. I don't know. I can't remember. I can't remember.

GABRIEL That's all right. It's all right.

CLIFF Oh yes. Of course, it's all right. Everything is all right. This is a very beautiful place. I love gardens. I would have liked to have been a gardener. If things had panned out different. To what they have.

GABRIEL It is a beautiful garden. This place used to be some kind of stately home, belonging to one of those aristocratic English families. Now it's a State Institution. That's the way it goes.

CLIFF It is. Eternal flux. So you want to be a lawyer?

GABRIEL Yes. Or even a barrister. That's my real ambition.

CLIFF That's excellent. Education is the key to everything. I've had some experience of The Law. Like, I've been in court an' that. Several times.

GABRIEL I know you have.

CLIFF Anything you want to know about the Law and you come to me. My name is Clifford.

Danelaw

GABRIEL I will.

CLIFF I like barristers and lawyers. But I don't like judges.

GABRIEL No. I can understand why that would be the case.

CLIFF This last judge I had was a woman. And I don't agree with that. Women judges. I find women judges to be too moralistic. They lack true insight into the chaotic mystery of the human heart. They do mine anyway. She told me I was a racist thug! And that there was no place for me in society. Which I think is demonstrably untrue. I'm here, aren't I? This is still society, isn't it?

GABRIEL Yes, indeed, it is.

CLIFF So there is a place for me. There is a place for me after all. Lying old cow. Yeh, she told me I was a racist. And it's not true. I don't think I am. I thought it was a crass and simplistic remark. It's women, you see: they don't have any judgement. I love people. I love the whole world. I always have done. Well, until I was about ten or eleven. Then, it's true, I did embark on what I call my Disillusioned Phase, when there were some nasty incidents, it's true, when I ended up murdering some people. But that all in the past, that is. I'm back on track now. This is a new dawn for all humanity. She couldn't see that. Because she was a hatchet-faced old bitch with hostile, moralistic, frosty blue eyes! She wore glasses in octagonal frames. I mean!

Act Two – Scene Ten

GABRIEL I know. I know, mate. It's all right. Calm down. Shhhh!

CLIFF And now I am here. In a beautiful garden. With my friend. *(Pause. Holds out dog)* Doggie. *(As a noun)* Woof-woof. *(Pause)* I remember the farm very clearly. Granddad used to work on it as a young man. He went back to it after the war. Then he retired and went to live in a council flat in Chelmsford. *(Pause)* I love Chelmsford. *(Pause)* Granddad took me to visit the farm sometimes. And he also took me to see a great big spreading oak tree in the middle of a corn field, under which he first fucked our Nanna! On August the fifteenth, nineteen thirty-four, at three o'clock in the afternoon. Surrounded by the standing sheaves of corn. It was where he made Daddy. *(Pause)* Poor Daddy. He started in a corn field in Essex and he died in a mental hospital in Friern Barnet. Yeh. *(Pause)* I use my time here wisely. I don't mix with the other guests. I stand aloof. *(Pause)* And I had a wonderful dream about Mr. Warboys! I was with Mr. Warboys in the back of his 1938 Rolls Royce. It was a beautiful summer's day and the top was down and we were bowling silently along ... somewhere on the South Downs, I think ... and we were sitting side by side together on red leather seats. And there was a big picnic hamper between us and we were feasting on chicken legs and drinking champagne and I turned to Mr. Warboys and smiled at him and he burst into joyous laughter! I was happy. There was sunshine in my heart. And then Mr. Warboys called out to the chauffeur 'Drive straight on to the Clifton, Milburn! We'll stay there forever!' And the driver turned round with a smile and said 'Very good, Sir!' And it was that Alan Milburn! Him who used to be Health Secretary! *(Pause)* And then, I was on this old blue Fordson Major tractor. It was harvest time and I drove it to the cornfield in Essex where Granddad first fucked our Nanna under the big oak tree. And I climbed into the oak tree – the great big ancient oak that had stood at the centre of England for centuries – and I looked out over the standing sheaves of corn and I impaled myself on the tree! For my people. That's all I ever wanted to do – serve my people. And I hung there for nine days and nine nights and my blood ran into the ground for my people that they should live my blood ran into the ground ... and I blessed Rowena my dear dear friend from so long ago and my blood ran into the ground. And for you too my brother Jason I sent my thoughts out to you to where I could see you riding a horse in beautiful countryside. And my blood ran into the ground for you and for everyone my blood ran into the ground. And on the last night a great big full shining moon came up over the silent sheaves of corn. And the ancient kingdom of *DANELAW* was established again. Just like it was and always will be, for ever and ever. *(Pause)* And my name is Odin now. Yeh. Odin. I want you to call me Odin. *(Starts to move off SR, but GABRIEL guides him SL)*

Act Two – Scene Ten

GABRIEL This way, Odin.

CLIFF Oh. Sorry.

GABRIEL No problem.

> *Exit both SL*
>
> *FADE TO BLACK*

THE END.

www.ingramcontent.com/pod-product-compliance
Lightning Source LLC
Chambersburg PA
CBHW051707040426
42446CB00008B/762